# Understanding
# Buddhism

Don Nardo

San Diego, CA

© 2019 ReferencePoint Press, Inc.
Printed in the United States

**For more information, contact:**
ReferencePoint Press, Inc.
PO Box 27779
San Diego, CA 92198
www.ReferencePointPress.com

LIBRARY OF CONGRESS CATALOGING-IN-PUBLICATION DATA

Name: Nardo, Don, 1947– author.
Title: Understanding Buddhism/by Don Nardo.
Description: San Diego: ReferencePoint Press, 2018. | Series: Understanding World Religions series | Includes bibliographical references and index.
Identifiers: LCCN 2017053658 (print) | LCCN 2018018168 (ebook) | ISBN 9781682824603 (eBook) | ISBN 9781682824597 (hardback)
Subjects: LCSH: Buddhism.
Classification: LCC BQ4022 (ebook) | LCC BQ4022 .N37 2018 (print) | DDC 294.3—dc23
LC record available at https://lccn.loc.gov/2017053658

# CONTENTS

# World Religions: By the Numbers

According to a 2017 Pew Research Center demographic analysis, Christians were the largest religious group in the world in 2015. However, that may be changing. The same analysis projects Muslims to be the world's fastest-growing major religious group over the next four decades.

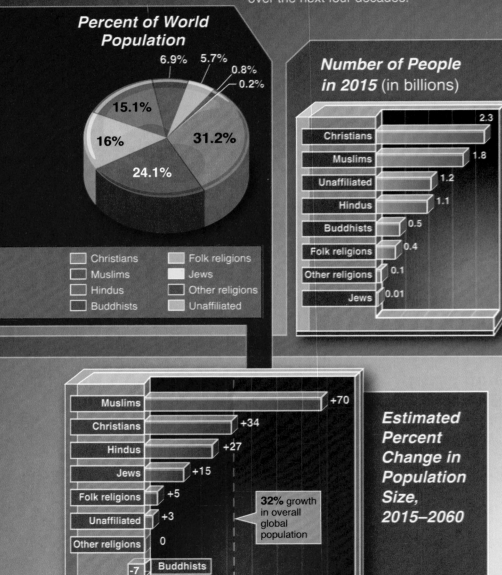

## Percent of World Population

- 6.9%
- 5.7%
- 0.8%
- 0.2%
- 15.1%
- 16%
- 31.2%
- 24.1%

Legend:
- Christians
- Muslims
- Hindus
- Buddhists
- Folk religions
- Jews
- Other religions
- Unaffiliated

## Number of People in 2015 (in billions)

- Christians: 2.3
- Muslims: 1.8
- Unaffiliated: 1.2
- Hindus: 1.1
- Buddhists: 0.5
- Folk religions: 0.4
- Other religions: 0.1
- Jews: 0.01

## Estimated Percent Change in Population Size, 2015–2060

- Muslims: +70
- Christians: +34
- Hindus: +27
- Jews: +15
- Folk religions: +5
- Unaffiliated: +3
- Other religions: 0
- Buddhists: -7

**32%** growth in overall global population

Source: Conrad Hackett and David McClendon, "Christians Remain World's Largest Religious Group, but They Are Declining in Europe," Pew Research Center: The Changing Global Religious Landscape, April 5, 2017. www.pewresearch.org.

# Buddhism: Religion or Philosophy?

In 1967 famed American civil rights leader Martin Luther King Jr. nominated Thích Nhất Hạnh for the prestigious Nobel Peace Prize. Born in Vietnam in 1926, Nhất Hạnh was then, and still is, widely seen as one of the world's leading Buddhist teachers. He has lectured on Buddhism around the globe, including at New York's Columbia University, and written dozens of widely popular books. In nominating him, King remarked, "I do not personally know of anyone more worthy of this prize than this gentle monk from Vietnam. His ideas for peace, if applied, would build a monument to . . . world brotherhood, to humanity."[1]

In fact, Nhất Hạnh had dedicated his entire life to denouncing war and promoting world peace. One of his most widely admired teachings states, "Aware of the suffering created by fanaticism and intolerance, we are determined not to be [bound] to any doctrine, theory, or ideology, even Buddhist ones. Buddhist teachings are guiding means to help us learn to look deeply and to develop our understanding and compassion. They are not doctrines to fight, kill, or die for."[2]

This last statement might be surprising to people of other faiths. Throughout history Christians, Jews, and Muslims have fought and died to promote or defend their faiths. What makes Buddhism so different?

## The Buddha Was Only a Man

Buddhism is the world's fourth-largest religion, after Christianity, Islam, and Hinduism. In 2017 there were more than 500 million Buddhists, together making up about 7 percent of the global population. Most Buddhists dwell in Asia. Of the nations on that vast continent, China has the most Buddhists, numbering roughly

Vietnamese monk Thích Nhất Hạnh (pictured) has for decades been viewed as one of the world's leading authorities on Buddhism. He has stated that Buddhist teachings are means by which humans can develop understanding and compassion.

240 million—about 18 percent of that country's population. Still, there are Buddhists all over the planet, even if in smaller numbers. Around 4 million live in North America, for instance, and about 1.3 million in Europe. Moreover, the faith is slowly but constantly growing in popularity, especially in Western nations.

Buddhists follow the teachings of the Buddha. The Buddha was a man, not a god. In fact, Siddhartha Gautama, the Indian-born prince who later became the Buddha, or "Enlightened One," repeatedly informed his followers that he was not a divine savior or deity. He was a thinker and teacher who had found a viable path to wisdom and inner peace and wanted to help others trod that same path.

Moreover, Buddhism does not recognize an all-powerful god who created the universe and provides guidance to humanity. Instead, the Buddha preached that such a deity does not exist. Humanity is on its own, and each individual must learn to be his or her own guide in life. In the words of American Buddhist writer Nicholas Liusuwan, "The Buddha's teachings emphasized personal practice and adhering to moral principles above any kind of dogma [strict religious creed or belief system]. Even in regards to the [core Buddhist teachings], the Buddha doesn't describe them as divine laws, but as practical guidelines to follow for one's own happiness."[3]

## An Unrelenting Quest

For these reasons, Liusuwan adds, "a common debate among people in modern times, especially among Westerners, is that Buddhism is not a religion, but a philosophy or way of life."[4] Reflecting this philosophical dimension of Buddhism is the fact that at its core, it is a kind of unrelenting quest. The searchers seek to find and embrace wisdom, kindness, compassion, and moral behavior. Moreover, by striving to live by the precepts of kindness, compassion, and morality, a devout Buddhist accepts and practices nonviolence. That is why Nhất Hạnh chose to devote most of his time and energies to antiwar activities.

Still, Nhất Hạnh, Liusuwan, and other dedicated Buddhists do acknowledge that their faith is, at least in some ways, also a religion. First, it is in many ways organized like other religions. For example, Buddhism has highly esteemed writings (called scriptures in most faiths), priests, and temples. Also, many Buddhists pray—although Buddhist prayers are more a form of meditation than a request for divine guidance or relief. In addition, most Buddhists believe in an afterlife. There, they say, the essences of deceased enlightened humans live on for eternity. Furthermore, numerous Buddhists accept the notion of reincarnation—that after death people return to earth in either human or animal form. Concepts and practices like these are part of many religions.

Buddhism therefore features both philosophical and religious aspects. As a result, there may never be a definitive answer to the question of whether it is a philosophy or a religion. Liusuwan explains, "There are those who firmly believe Buddhism is a religion and those who firmly believe it is a philosophy." In the end, he says, "each side has their own points, and it is a legitimate debate with solid arguments both ways depending on how one defines religion."[5]

One thing is certain. Whether motivated by the philosophical or religious facets of Buddhism, devoted adherents like Nhất Hạnh continue to work tirelessly for the betterment of humanity. This is what the Buddha did, they point out, and they are driven to follow his example.

# CHAPTER ONE

# The Origins of Buddhism

The beginnings of one of the world's largest faiths—Buddhism—lie in the now shadowy mists of sixth-century-BCE India. In those days that vast region was rocked by political turmoil, making life unstable and uncertain for large numbers of people. Numerous villages, towns, and small cities dominated by local tribes were steadily giving way to sprawling, populous kingdoms ruled by powerful monarchs.

## A Sheltered Life

In one of those kingdoms—Lumbini, lying just south of the towering Himalaya Mountains (in what is now Nepal)—a new royal prince was born in about 563 BCE. His father, King Shuddhodhana, named him Siddhartha. In the local language, Sanskrit, the child's name means "a man who achieves his goals." No one then realized how prophetic this name would turn out to be. Neither young Siddhartha's relatives nor their subjects could have foreseen that he would one day become the Buddha, the founder of a new faith practiced by millions of people.

The only thing that King Shuddhodhana knew, or at least thought he knew, about his son's future came from some palace holy men who advised the ruler in spiritual matters. They claimed that in a vision they saw that the boy's life had two possible outcomes. If he spent all his days within the palace walls, he would someday become a carefree and happy ruler. In contrast, if he went outside the palace and into the outside world, he would eventually become a poverty-stricken, lonely hermit.

Hearing this prophecy, the king went to great lengths to try to keep the second part from coming to pass. He posted dozens of guards whose special task was to make sure that young Siddhartha stayed inside the palace walls at all times. From infancy to young manhood, therefore, the prince led a sheltered life filled with creature comforts, laughter, and all manner of luxuries. He had no inkling of what the outside world was like. He knew nothing of disease, suffering, and death. Later, as an old man, he was said to have looked back on his childhood and teen years and said:

> I was delicate, excessively delicate. In my father's dwelling three lotus ponds were made purposely for me. Blue lotuses bloomed in one, red in another, and white in the third. [Day and] night a white parasol was held over me so that I might not be touched by heat or cold, dust, leaves, or dew. [I was regularly] entertained by female musicians, without coming down from the palace.[6]

## The Prince's Shocking Discovery

Siddhartha's life of privilege and bliss continued on into his twenties. He married a lovely young princess named Yasodhara, and they had a son together, whom they named Rahula. The three continually enjoyed good health and were extremely happy.

This contented existence came to a sudden halt, however, when Siddhartha was twenty-nine. For years he had wondered about the world beyond the palace walls. Finally, his curiosity got the better of him. With the aid of a faithful servant, the prince managed to get past the guards and secretly escaped into the countryside.

Less than an hour after gaining his freedom, the prince found himself in a rural village and encountered a sight he had never before beheld. It was a very old man with a wrinkled face, white hair, and a body emaciated from not having enough to eat. Siddhartha later recalled

*"[Day and] night a white parasol was held over me so that I might not be touched by heat or cold, dust, leaves, or dew."[6]*
—The Buddha

This painting depicts Siddhartha—who later became the Buddha—encountering sickness, old age, and death for the first time after living a sheltered life. This incident led him to the realization that human existence is filled with suffering.

thinking at that moment, "I, too, am subject to old age." He wondered whether he should be "troubled, ashamed, and disgusted" at the sight of the ancient villager? "This seemed to me not fitting," the prince told himself. "As I thus reflected, all the [joy of] my youth suddenly disappeared."[7]

Very soon after that, Siddhartha came upon two other sights he had never encountered—a sick person and a corpse. The deceased's relatives were carrying the body through the local streets on their way to the graveyard. Shocked, the prince asked his servant if disease and death were common in Indian society and elsewhere. The servant told him that indeed, sickness was widespread in everyday life across the known world. He also told his master that death was the inevitable end for all living things, including people.

## Enduring Physical Punishment

Siddhartha for the first time realized one of life's main truths—that the world is full of suffering. But, he asked himself, why does suffering exist? Also, was there perhaps a way to avoid it? Mere seconds after he had considered these queries, a holy man strode by. The servant explained to Siddhartha that such monks often sought out deserted, quiet places and meditated for long periods in hopes of discovering life's deeper meanings. The prince considered this idea. Maybe if he, too, devoted himself to solitude and meditation, he could understand some of the many realities of life he had missed while trapped in his father's palace.

It also struck the young man that his becoming a solitary monk would require leaving behind his relatives, among them his wife and son, whom he dearly loved. He felt he could not leave them without saying good-bye. So that night, he sneaked back into the palace. He stood over them and bade them farewell in silence as they slept.

Away from the palace again, Siddhartha abandoned all his luxuries and even got rid of most of his clothes. Eager to begin meditating and gaining wisdom, he did what many monks did—began practicing extreme self-discipline and self-denial. Week after strenuous week, he endured extremes of heat and cold in hopes of better learning to focus his mind and think deep thoughts. He no longer washed. Also, at times he lay for hours on tangles of thorns and slept beside rotting human corpses that had been tossed into a mass grave. Worst of all, he ate less and less and finally tried to live on a single grain of rice each day. After a while, he got so thin that when he pressed a hand to his stomach he could feel his spine. "The bones of my spine," he later remembered, "were like a row of spindles."[8]

> "The bones of my spine were like a row of spindles."[8]
> —The Buddha

As in the cases of many other founders of faiths, later fanciful stories grew up about the Buddha. One says that Siddhartha's mother, Queen Maya, was implanted with her son's seed by miraculous means. Supposedly, in her sleep she dreamed that a sacred white elephant entered her chamber. A passage in the *Jataka*, some fifth-century-CE birth tales about the Buddha, states that in its trunk, the creature "held a white lotus [flower]. Trumpeting, he entered the golden mansion, made a right-wise circle three times around [Maya's] bed, smote [struck] her right side, and appeared to enter her womb." The next morning, Maya awakened and told her husband, the king, about the dream. He called together some monks and asked them to explain what the dream meant. They concluded that the white elephant was a sign that the queen was now pregnant. Moreover, the child would be a boy possessing special insights about the world. Not long afterward, other omens occurred. In one, a bright light blazed in the night sky while Maya was sleeping. In addition, several deaf people regained their hearing, and some physically disabled people were suddenly able to walk.

Quoted in E.J. Thomas, *The Life of Buddha in Legend and History.* London: Kegan Paul, 2003, pp. 31–32.

All of this self-punishment eventually turned out to be pointless, Siddhartha learned. Torturing himself this way did not help him find life's truths and attain a state of enlightenment, or great wisdom. In fact, he later said, a seeker of wisdom should "be moderate. Let him eat and drink according to the needs of the body." Keeping "the body in good health is a duty, for otherwise we shall not be able to trim the lamp of [attain] wisdom, and keep our mind strong and clear."[9]

## A Newly Awakened Intellect

As near as modern scholars can tell, Siddhartha was around thirty-five when he began eating normally again. He also washed himself thoroughly and put on clean clothes. Within a few months he had regained his health and felt ready to try once more to attain great wisdom and discover the cause of human suffering.

Sometime in the late spring of 528 BCE, the earnest young seeker of life's truths was walking through a wide, lush meadow and noticed a lone banyan tree. Beneath its branches he sat down to rest and meditate. He had no way of knowing that it would later become famous and revered as the Bodhi Tree, or "Tree of Wisdom."

Siddhartha now meditated so intently that he entered into a trancelike state in which he was able to clear his mind of all thoughts unrelated to his special intellectual quest. While in this state, he closely examined concepts like unhappiness, illness, old age, and death and their meaning to humanity. "I saw beings passing away and being reborn, low and high," he later recalled. Some of those beings were happy, while others dwelled in abject misery. He said that his intellectual journey was guided by an abiding belief in the "universal law by which every act of good or evil will be rewarded or punished in this life or in some later incarnation of the soul."[10]

> *"I saw beings passing away and being reborn, low and high."*[10]
> —The Buddha

At about age thirty-five, Siddhartha sat down under a banyan tree to rest and meditate. When he emerged from his meditation, he had realized the reasons for human suffering, thereby becoming the Buddha, or the Enlightened One.

Exactly how long Siddhartha meditated beneath the Bodhi Tree will never be known. It might have been many days. However long he remained at a level of concentration deeper than any human had ever experienced, he eventually managed to return to waking consciousness. According to tradition, he opened his eyes on May 25, 528 BCE. Behind those eyes now resided a newly awakened intellect of astonishing breadth and depth. The former Prince Siddhartha had finally realized the reasons for human suffering and thereby had been transformed into the Buddha, the Enlightened One (or Awakened One).

## Beyond All Life and Death

The Buddha now realized that human suffering is very often the result of arrogance, greed, and self-indulgence. People with those traits usually think primarily of their own comforts and tend to collect material goods to maintain those comforts, he concluded. In the meantime, they give less and less thought to treating others justly and to eradicating poverty and human misery. He also realized that conceit and greed and the ills they bring about are not inevitable. Well-meaning people *can* overcome them, he said, and he conceived of a means of doing just that. It is a code, or system, of righteous conduct and rules that he called the Eightfold Path, or Middle Way.

A few weeks after envisioning these profound concepts, the Buddha decided to share them with others. First he sought out five monks whom he had briefly encountered in his travels. As he approached them, they immediately noticed that he had changed. They detected something noble about his demeanor and a look of high intelligence in his eyes. Sitting down with them, he told them, "I have the way to [ultimate wisdom]. Let me tell you, let me teach you. And if you listen and learn and practice as I tell you, very soon you will know for yourselves, not in some future life but here and now in this present lifetime, that what I say is true. You will realize for yourself the state [of goodness] that is beyond all life and death."[11]

The five monks eagerly accepted the Buddha's teachings and thereby became his first five followers. He gathered many more devotees in the months and years that followed as the news of his enlightenment spread through northern India. In village after

As he approached death, the Buddha advised his followers not to spend time mourning him but instead to further knowledge about how to conquer suffering and how to lead a righteous life. One of his main teachings was that people shape their own destinies with their thoughts and actions.

village, people crowded around him and begged him to teach them what he had discovered about the meaning of life, death, goodness, and justice. He was glad to do so and delivered count-less lectures in which he urged people—both rich and poor—to avoid greed and the other ills that caused human suffering. If they followed the Middle Way and exhibited decent, moral behavior at all times, such misery would begin to disappear.

## His Childhood Home

The Buddha traveled onward, along with his growing legion of followers, for a few years. Eventually, they came to Lumbini, the kingdom in which he had been born as Prince Siddhartha. His father still ruled there. The king had heard about his son's spiritual transformation and was impressed that he had gained such a large following. Shuddhodhana therefore invited the Buddha to visit his family and childhood home.

When the visiting celebrity arrived at the palace, the king warmly embraced him and told him how proud of him he was. Then the Buddha caught sight of his wife and son, who was now a young man. The former Siddhartha was surprised to learn that

In the centuries following the Buddha's death, numerous tales emerged about his life and his relationship with his family members, including his son, Rahula. Modern experts say that telling the real stories from the fictional ones is now often difficult. In one of these anecdotes, the Buddha tries to instill in his son the importance of always thinking before acting—as a way to make fewer mistakes.

> [The Buddha asked:] "What do you think about this, Rahula? What is the purpose of a mirror?"
>
> [The boy answered:] "The purpose of a mirror is to look at yourself."
>
> [The Buddha responded:] "Even so, Rahula, one should act with body, speech, or mind only after first looking at oneself. Before acting with body, speech, or mind, one should think: 'What I am about to do, will it harm me or others?' If you can answer: 'Yes, it will,' then you should not act. But if you can answer: 'No, it will not,' then you should act. You should reflect in the same way while acting and after having acted. Therefore, Rahula, you should train yourself thinking: 'We will act only after repeatedly looking at ourselves, only after reflecting on ourselves.'"

Quoted in Buddha Dharma Education Association, "Rahula, the Son of the Enlightened One," 2008. www .buddhanet.net.

both of them were well acquainted with his teachings and had already become followers. Indeed, Rahula declared that he himself had abandoned court politics and the chance to someday become king and was ready to join his father in his efforts to teach people about the Middle Way.

Accompanied by his son and many other loyal adherents, the Buddha continued traveling and teaching for several more decades. It was said that in the year 483 BCE, when he was about eighty, he sensed his own death approaching. Soon, he was too old and weak to trek any further and took to his bed. On his last day of life, he spoke to the dozens of admirers who now crowded around him and advised them not to spend needless time mourning his passing. Rather, he said, they should use their time and energy to further spread knowledge about suffering, how to conquer it, and how to lead righteous lives.

Supposedly, with his final breath the Buddha said, "Decay is inherent in all things. Work out your own salvation with diligence."[12] In this way, he reminded his followers that each person's destiny is shaped mostly by his or her own thoughts and actions. He or she can learn to both live and die as a good person who respects others and treats them justly. Summing up the Buddha's enormous influence on large sectors of humanity during many generations, the late modern Indian statesman and philosopher Sarvepalli Radhakrishnan wrote, "He belongs to the history of the world's thought, to the general inheritance of all cultivated men. For, judged by intellectual integrity, moral earnestness, and spiritual insight, he is undoubtedly one of the greatest figures in history."[13]

> *"[The Buddha] is undoubtedly one of the greatest figures in history."*[13]
>
> —Modern Indian statesman and philosopher Sarvepalli Radhakrishnan

# CHAPTER TWO

# The Faith Spreads Far and Wide

In the centuries immediately following the Buddha's passing in about 483 BCE, the philosophical-religious movement he had started spread across large portions of Asia. This process began the year of his death. Although deeply saddened by the loss of their spiritual leader, many of his followers were eager to honor his memory by continuing to spread his teachings.

## The Early Buddhist Councils

With that goal in mind, a mere three months after the Buddha's death, about five hundred of his most devout adherents held a meeting. It later came to be known as the First Buddhist Council, sometimes called the Council of Rajir, after the northern Indian town where it was held. It was understood that during their travels, they would spread the Buddha's *sutras*, or sayings, by word of mouth. (Very few people could read at the time, and books were very rare.)

At the meeting, therefore, it was agreed that everyone should preach the same sutras, which should be as close to the Buddha's own words as possible. Hence, they turned to Ananda, the Enlightened One's cousin, who had joined the movement thirty years before. He had been quite close to the Buddha and had an excellent memory. Over the course of days, Ananda recited every sutra he had ever heard his master say, while the rest of those present listened intently. They then rehearsed those sayings over and over.

After disbanding, these initial Buddhist missionaries went their separate ways and slowly made their way into other parts of India. A few even ventured somewhat beyond its borders. They did their best to maintain Buddhist doctrine (ideals, sayings, and rules). But as the decades passed, some naturally began interpreting the Buddha's words in their own ways.

Thus, when the Second Buddhist Council was held about a century after the first, it was clear that a schism, or rupture, had taken place in the Buddhists' ranks. In the years following that conference, the new faith split into two general groups. One, made up of conservative traditionalists, felt that all teachings should focus strictly on the Buddha's original ideas and words. They became known as Theravada Buddhists, or the Theravada. The other group's members believed that new interpretations of some Buddhist ideals was natural and healthy. They became known as Mahayana Buddhists, or the Mahayana. (Later, other splinter groups separated from these main ones, eventually producing almost twenty distinct schools of Buddhist thought.)

## An Astonishing Transformation

During the first two centuries of Buddhist expansion, the teachers, who called themselves monks, managed to bring the Buddha's ideas to much of India and a few nearby regions. The next phase of the faith's expansion was much larger. Moreover, it was spearheaded by a single, very popular and influential individual. His name was Ashoka, and he was ruler of the sprawling, powerful northern Indian kingdom of Magadha.

Like his grandfather and father before him, Ashoka, who became raja, or king, in the mid-260s BCE, began as a military monarch whose goal was to conquer other lands. The new ruler almost immediately set his sights on defeating the kingdom of Kalinga, lying along the Bay of Bengal, in east-central India. Ashoka's army was huge and well trained, so it made short work of the Kalingan forces. By 260 BCE Kalinga had been completely overwhelmed and most of its major towns ravaged and/or burned. According to Ashoka's own public records, 100,000 Kalingans were killed and another 150,000 left homeless.

Ashoka's victory was only one of many brutal conquests in ancient times. It would not have been nearly as important in later history books if it had not been for this conqueror's subsequent astonishing transformation. After Ashoka journeyed through

In the mid-260s BCE, the Indian ruler Ashoka (pictured) underwent a personal transformation from fierce warrior to pacifist. This prompted him to convert to Buddhism and advocate its nonviolent ideals.

Kalinga to survey the damage his army had done, he was suddenly overcome with sadness and distress. The reasons for this reaction remain unknown. Some historians speculate that up till then, he was an idealistic young man who thought the war would be a romantic, adventurous contest among brave warriors. Now, the raja saw firsthand that his soldiers had slaughtered thousands of innocent women and children and inflicted human suffering on an immense scale.

For whatever reason that Ashoka came to regret his conquest of Kalinga, his major change of heart soon provided an enormous boost to the still small-scale Buddhist movement. In large part this was because the Buddhists were pacifists who urged all people to refrain from violence. Ashoka now found himself in that very frame of mind, one that was rare in the ancient world. To inform his subjects of his new pacifist feelings, he sent messengers far and wide to convey his words, which stated in part, "[I am] deeply pained by the killing, dying, and deportation that take place when an unconquered country is conquered. . . . These misfortunes befall all (as a result of war), and this pains [me]. . . . Therefore the killing, death, or deportation of a hundredth, or even a thousandth part of those who died during the conquest of Kalinga now pains [me]." Ashoka added that he now believed, as the Buddhists did, that it would be far more moral to adopt the principle of "non-injury, restraint and impartiality to all beings."[14]

"[I am] deeply pained by the killing, dying, and deportation that take place when an unconquered country is conquered."[14]

—Indian king Ashoka

## Respect for All Faiths

To have their formerly warlike raja abruptly renounce violence and war was surprising enough to most Magadhans. They were totally unprepared for his next move, which was to convert to Buddhism and completely dedicate himself to its ideals. At the time, most Magadhans and other Indians were Hindus, not Buddhists. In fact, Ashoka himself had been a Hindu all his life. But he knew that in spite of its many fine attributes as a faith, Hinduism did permit violent acts under certain circumstances. By contrast, Buddhism rejected all violent behavior in all situations.

By converting to Buddhism, therefore, Ashoka was able to create a powerful teaching moment for his subjects. He had his own versions of various Buddhist principles carved into stone monuments across northern India. He also urged Buddhists in Magadha to explain their beliefs to his non-Buddhist subjects. No

The Buddhist movement split into two major factions in the years following the Second Buddhist Council. These groups—the Theravada and Mahayana—were alike in many ways. But they differed on a number of technical issues. For example, the conservative Theravada insisted on using only the Buddha's original teachings when preaching. In contrast, the more progressive Mahayana used the original but also allowed the use of some later Buddhist sayings and ideas. Another difference concerned the issue of attaining enlightenment. The Theravada said that reaching that goal should be a person's sole task in life. But the Mahayana felt that a person should also make a serious effort to help other sentient (knowing/feeling) beings find happiness. In addition, the Mahayana strongly stressed being a vegetarian (although they did not make it compulsory), whereas the Theravada held that being a vegetarian was unnecessary. Still another difference was where to worship. The Theravada said it was fitting to worship anywhere, as long as one kept the Buddha and his teachings in mind. The Mahayana, in comparison, preferred to use an elaborate temple containing images of the Buddha and other individuals who had attained enlightenment.

Hindus, nor anyone else, were forced to convert to Buddhism, however. In fact, Ashoka firmly stressed the importance of religious toleration, advocating that all religions should be respected. In one of his carved edicts, he explained that when one honors all faiths,

> one's own religion benefits, and so do other religions, while doing otherwise harms one's own religion and the religions of others. Whoever praises his own religion, due to excessive devotion, and condemns others with the thought "Let me glorify my own religion," only harms his own religion. Therefore contact (between religions) is good. One should listen to and respect the doctrines professed by others.[15]

As a result of this and other progressive policies Ashoka instituted, Buddhists gained almost instant respect in large sectors of India. After learning about Buddhist beliefs, some Hindus followed the raja's example and converted to Buddhism. However, although a majority of Indians remained Hindus, many of them saw certain values in the Buddha's teachings. They managed to reconcile Buddhist ideals of justice and nonviolence with existing Hindu concepts of belief in multiple gods. In this way, thanks to Ashoka, large numbers of Hindu Indians incorporated some Buddhist principles into their traditional belief system.

## The Power of the Buddhist Message

Ashoka also significantly aided the Buddhists' movement by helping them spread their ideas far beyond India's borders. Employing the considerable resources he enjoyed as a wealthy king, he sent well-trained Buddhist missionaries to numerous other Asian lands. Members of these bold expeditions eventually reached and affected the destinies of Korea, China, Cambodia, Thailand, and Japan, among many others. Almost all of the Buddhist missions established in these places took root and over time blossomed, transforming the local societies.

*"Herein lies the greatness of Ashoka."* [16]

—Historian R.K. Mookerji

Indeed, Buddhism still owes Ashoka an immeasurable debt. More than any other single person, he made it possible for that faith to become a worldwide religion. As historian R.K. Mookerji puts it, "Herein lies the greatness of Ashoka. No victorious monarch in the history of the world is known to have ever [accomplished] anything like it." [16]

Yet while Ashoka provided the means for Buddhists to take their message to diverse regions, ultimately it was the power and popularity of that message that made people in those lands embrace it. Without doubt, critical to this success was the fact that much of Buddhism is a philosophy and way of viewing life, death, and morality. People saw that they could accept various Buddhist principles without giving up their traditional religions. Just as a number of Indian Hindus had, at first some residents of other Asian lands worked such principles into their existing faiths. Later, over the course of decades, or in some cases centuries, larger and larger sectors of those societies converted completely to Buddhism.

The adoption of Buddhism did not always happen gradually, however. In a few places Ashoka's missionaries had an immediate and major impact and won over entire populations in short

This mural scene depicts the daughter of Ashoka, Sanghamitta. Together with her brother, Mahinda, she traveled to the island nation of what is today Sri Lanka to spread the teachings of Buddhism.

Of the Indo-Greek kings who converted to Buddhism, the best known is Menander (reigned ca. 165–130 BCE), whom the ancient Indians called Milinda. The ancient Buddhist text titled *Milindapanha*, or "The Questions of King Milinda," dating to about 100 BCE, purports to record a conversation between Menander and a Buddhist holy man named Nagasena. Supposedly, the king is considering converting to Buddhism and asks the monk a series of questions about Buddhist beliefs. The following brief excerpt captures the flavor of the text.

The king said: "What, Nagasena, is the characteristic mark of wisdom?"

[Nagasena answers "enlightenment."]

"And how is enlightenment its mark?"

"When wisdom springs up in the heart, O king, it dispels the darkness of ignorance, it causes the radiance of knowledge to arise, it makes the light of intelligence to shine forth, and it makes the Noble Truths plain." . . .

"Give me an illustration."

"It is like a lamp, O king, which a man might introduce into a house in darkness. When the lamp had been brought in, it would dispel the darkness [and] make the objects there plainly visible. Just so would wisdom in a man have such effects."

"Well put, Nagasena!"

T.W. Rys Davids, trans., *The Questions of King Milinda*. New York: Dover, 1963, pp. 61–62.

order. Usually key to this was the initial and rapid conversion of the country's ruler. That set an example for the ruler's subjects to follow. This is what happened in Sri Lanka (formerly Ceylon), the island nation situated southeast of India. Ashoka sent his own son and daughter—recent converts to Buddhism—to Sri Lanka. There they quickly won over the king, Tissa, along with his entire royal court. These nobles then introduced Buddhism to Tissa's subjects, most of whom converted in the space of only a few years. Buddhism remains the dominant faith of Sri Lanka.

Even while the Sri Lankans were accepting the Buddha's teachings, further north, in the vast region of China, Buddhist monks were preaching and setting up monasteries. There is some dispute among modern experts about exactly when and how Buddhism first took root in China. Some scholars think that a few Buddhist monks arrived there even before Ashoka sent out his missionaries in the third century BCE. Another view is that the missionaries first converted people along the so-called Silk Road, the age-old trade route stretching from southwestern China into what are now Iran and Iraq. Then the faith spread eastward along that route and into China.

It is possible that both of these scenarios occurred. The fact is that Buddhism initially developed slowly in China, in fits and starts, as some Chinese emperors saw it as a threat to local traditions and tried to eradicate it. These attempts were always unsuccessful, and Buddhism eventually became one of China's principal faiths and philosophical systems.

## The Silk Road and the Greeks

While Buddhist monks struggled to spread their ideas among the Chinese, those ideas slowly but steadily moved westward along the Silk Road. As they made their way through what are now Afghanistan and northern Iran, merchants, travelers, and mission-aries alike encountered numerous thriving and often competing cultures. Only a few included Afghan herders and farmers; poly-theistic tribes making up the Parthian Empire, centered in Iran; and colonies of Greek soldiers who had settled in the region af-ter Greek conqueror Alexander the Great's empire (which briefly stretched into India) fell apart in the late 300s BCE.

These and other groups along the Silk Road all felt the influ-ence of Buddhist monks in the second and first centuries BCE or somewhat later. In part by displaying recently written Buddhist texts (the first known Buddhist literature), the monks managed to convert some of the local rulers. In turn, these wealthy individuals helped the monks establish monasteries, temples, and places for Buddhists to rest and meditate. Archaeologists have found the

In the second and first centuries BCE, Buddhist monks established places along the Silk Road in China where travelers could meditate and rest. The art shown here is located at such a site, one in a series of caves that are well known for their wall paintings.

ruins of such sites, often in caves, in the region's sometimes bleak hills and deserts. According to Smithsonian Institution scholars Azim Nanji and Sarfaroz Niyozov:

Along the Silk Road there were kings and rulers who sought to rise above certain groups, tribes, and religious traditions. [They] built monasteries and temples along the

Silk Road that were often used by the faithful of various religions [including Buddhism]. One such [Buddhist] monastery is believed to have been in the famous city of Bukhara, which later became a major Central Asian cultural center of Islam. [The] founding of monasteries and the rise of Buddhist [literature] produced favorable conditions for the general spread of Buddhism. Rulers, missionaries, monks, and traders all contributed to make Buddhism a very significant presence all over Central Asia.[17]

Of these Buddhist conversions along the Silk Road, perhaps none were more remarkable than those of the local Greeks. Originally they were polytheists (believers in multiple gods), like the Hindus and Iranian-based Parthians. The small kingdoms set up by Greek soldiers in the second and first centuries BCE in western India (now Pakistan) and Afghanistan proved very receptive to Buddhist ideas.

*"Rulers, missionaries, monks, and traders all contributed to make Buddhism a very significant presence all over Central Asia."[17]*

—Scholars Azim Nanji and Sarfaroz Niyozov

One reason for this was that, unlike their ancestors, who were born in faraway Greece, these were what modern scholars call Indo-Greeks. Several generations of them knew only the India-Afghanistan region as their home. As a result, not only did they introduce many Greek cultural ideas to the area, the area imparted to them many aspects of the local culture. This included Buddhism, which many local Greeks embraced. These conversions by the Indo-Greeks are noteworthy because they were the first Western (European-based) people early Buddhism encountered. They foreshadowed today's world, in which, after two millennia of relentless Buddhist expansion, every Western country has at least some followers of the Buddha within in its ranks.

# CHAPTER THREE

# What Do Buddhists Believe?

Many different sects—what Christians call denominations—of Buddhism exist in the modern world. Each has its own way of looking at the faith, as do the countless individuals who practice Buddhism. In the words of Boston College professor of Buddhism John Makransky, people must absorb Buddhist truths "through their own forms of thought, culture, and aesthetics, not in just one rigidly standardized way from a culture of origin."[18] Thus, Buddhists from China, Tibet, India, and the United States will each describe their faith and its beliefs in somewhat different ways.

The Buddha himself recognized that this element of individual understanding and interpretation would and should be part of any faith. One should not believe something "just because you have been told it," he said, "or because it is traditional." Moreover, "do not believe what your teacher tells you merely out of respect for the teacher. But whatsoever, after due examination and analysis, you find to be conducive to the good, the benefit, the welfare of all beings—that doctrine believe and cling to, and take as your guide."[19]

Still, certain central beliefs are more or less common to the vast majority of Buddhists around the globe. These are the faith's core teachings, which the Buddha established before his later followers added new and different interpretations of those basic ideas, along with writings of various kinds. Collectively, Buddhists call those original teachings Dharma (sometimes referred to as *the* Dharma).

## Four Noble Truths

According to Buddhist tradition, when the Buddha attained enlightenment, he suddenly recognized a set of fundamental truths about the universe and the human condition. These parts of the Dharma, which he called the Four Noble Truths, are among the most fundamental of all the faith's beliefs. Even he admitted that he did not need to become enlightened to know the first one, because it is self-evident. It is that life is full of suffering of various kinds.

In comparison, Buddhists believe that knowledge of the other three noble truths was the direct fruit of Buddha's achievement of enlightenment. The second truth identifies the primary causes of human suffering—namely conceit, self-indulgence, greed, and jealousy. These, the Buddha said, make people too concerned with their own needs and not enough with the needs of others. This situation naturally leads to treating others meanly, unjustly, and with disrespect—thereby creating misery and suffering.

The third great truth, the Buddha said, is that suffering is not inevitable but can be overcome or eradicated. As a spokesperson for the London-based Buddhist Society phrases it, suffering can be "brought to an end by transcending [the] strong sense of 'I' so that we come into greater harmony with things in general."[20] That is, people can eliminate human misery if they can find a way to switch their focus from just their own needs to those of others and society in general as well.

## Walking in the Middle Way

The natural question is: How can this positive change of focus be accomplished? The answer, according to the Buddha, was the fourth noble truth: Such constructive change can happen when people consistently practice good, or proper, behavior. Key to that practice is a code of conduct he called the Eightfold Path, or Middle Way. Its eight parts, as formulated by the Buddha, are right views (or understanding), right aspiration (or purpose), right speech, right behavior, right vocation (or livelihood), right effort, right thoughts (or awareness), and right contemplation (meaning concentration or meditation). An enlightened individual, the Buddha stated, has learned to "walk in the right path." It is one in which

> right views will be the torch to light his way. Right aspirations will be his guide. Right speech will be his dwelling-place on the road. His gait will be straight because it is

right behavior, his refreshments will be the right way of earning his livelihood. Right efforts will be his steps, right thoughts his breath, and right contemplation will give him the peace that follows in his footprints.[21]

People who follow the Eightfold Path will not only make others happier, the Buddha emphasized, they themselves will feel more contented. This is because practicing good behavior at all times

This stone sculpture is located in the Bangkok National Museum in Bangkok, Thailand. The wheel symbolizes Dharma, the Buddha's original teachings about the path to enlightenment.

naturally leads people to a happy state. If they speak the truth, are honest and just, and earn a living in a manner that does not harm others, they are on the path to enlightenment. People might eventually reach that lofty goal by managing to overcome their own suffering, along with the suffering of others. Having done that, they are liberated from life's woes and can achieve nirvana, a state of calmness, unselfishness, and harmony.

Thus, nirvana is not a place, like heaven, but a state of existence. What is more, someone who attains nirvana becomes a Buddha, a person possessed of great wisdom who always strives to do the right thing. Therefore, most Buddhists believe, in theory everyone has at least the potential to be as wise and admired a person as the original Buddha.

## Conduct to Be Avoided

The Buddha's early followers immediately grasped the wisdom and usefulness of the Eightfold Path. But a few of them made the point that all these steps are concerned with what people should do—that is, what constitutes good conduct. What about what people should *not* do, they asked him? Could he provide some examples of conduct that should always be avoided?

*"There are few evil deeds that a liar is incapable of committing."*[22]

—The Buddha

The Buddha's response to this question was a list that came to be known as the Five Moral Precepts (or Five Ethical Rules). One of them, more or less equivalent to "thou shall not kill" in Judaism and Christianity, states that one should never kill any living thing. A second Buddhist moral precept says that one should never steal. A third precept asserts that it is wrong to lie. In the words of a leading expert on Buddhism, Sunthorn Plamintr:

[This] precept, not to tell lies or resort to falsehood, is an important factor in social life and dealings. It concerns respect for truth. A respect for truth is a strong deterrent to inclinations or temptation to commit wrongful actions, while disregard for the same will only serve to encourage evil deeds. The Buddha has said: "There are few evil deeds that a liar is incapable of committing." The practice of [this] precept, therefore, helps to preserve one's credibility, trustworthiness, and honor.[22]

The last two moral precepts state that people should not commit any sort of sexual misconduct, nor consume intoxicating, or alcoholic, drinks.

No one questions the importance of following precepts against killing and stealing, of course. But at first glance, people who are unfamiliar with Buddhism at times get the impression that some of its other rules—especially the one against drinking alcohol—are overly strict. As Plamintr points out, however, the faith does

In this illustration from a nineteenth-century Buddhist text, a king who killed gazelles in a previous life and was reborn as a gazelle in a later life is himself being killed by hunters. One of Buddhism's Five Moral Precepts forbids the killing of any living thing.

not demand perfection. Rather, what is important is an honest *attempt* to follow all these precepts. He writes:

> It can hardly be expected that each and every practitioner will be able to follow them without committing the slightest error, any more than it can be expected of a music student not to make a single mistake in the course of his lessons. For people with certain temperaments or occupations, some precepts may appear more difficult to follow than the rest, but that should not be an obstacle to making an attempt to keep the precepts. If one is discouraged from practicing, one need simply consider that these precepts are a course of training; and training, by definition, implies imperfection and a gradual process of development.[23]

## No Monopoly on Truth

Another major aspect of the Buddhist belief system involves the concept and reality of divine beings like the God worshipped by Jews, Christians, and Muslims. First, the Buddha made a special point of telling his followers that he was not a god, nor did he possess any supernatural powers. Moreover, he outright dismissed the notion of humans performing miracles. According to historian Will Durant, he refused "to be drawn into any discussion about eternity, immortality, or God. The infinite is a myth, he said, a fiction of philosophers." In addition, the Buddha rejected the practice "of sacrificing to the gods, and looked with horror upon the slaughter of animals for these rites." Thus, Durant explains, "his conception of religion was purely ethical."[24]

Hence, according to the Buddha's original teachings, the world and humanity were not created by an all-powerful heavenly being who offers to save their souls. As a result, each person must find their own way to salvation. In Christianity and some other faiths, salvation consists of God forgiving people's sins and thereby allowing them to enter heaven after they die. In contrast, most Buddhists define salvation as an individual overcoming suffering and attaining true wisdom. In this manner, they can achieve the deliverance, or release, of nirvana.

# The Three Signs of Being

Buddhist tradition holds that by achieving enlightenment, the Buddha discovered an important cornerstone of the Buddhist belief system. It was the realization that everything in the physical world possesses three basic traits. He called them the Three Signs of Being, which are change, suffering, and I. According to the Buddhist Society, headquartered in London:

> The first [sign], change, points out the basic fact that nothing in the world is fixed or permanent. We ourselves are not the same people, either physically, emotionally or mentally, that we were... even ten minutes ago! Living as we do ... it is not possible for us to find lasting security. As regards the second sign, it was the experience of suffering that sent the Buddha off on his great spiritual quest. . . . Buddhists do believe that there is happiness in life, but know that it does not last and that even in the most fortunate of lives there is suffering.
>
> The third sign, I, what people call the human soul, is actually a collection of individual parts, each subject to constant change. There is no central core, so it is impermanent.

Buddhist Society, "Fundamental Teachings," 2017. www.thebuddhistsociety.org.

In part because each Buddhist is responsible for finding his or her own salvation, Buddhists as a whole view their beliefs as a very personal matter. No one expects or pressures his or her neighbor to strive for enlightenment, nor judges him or her for not striving for it. Therefore, Buddhists do not claim to have a monopoly on truth and tend not to see their faith as superior to other religions. In fact, most Buddhists acknowledge that their belief system, which lacks the concept of a supreme being, is not strictly a religion in the conventional sense. The late, widely respected Buddhist monk Narada Thera explained:

In Buddhism there is not, as in most other religions, an Almighty God to be obeyed and feared, [nor any] divine revelations or divine messengers. A Buddhist is, therefore, not subservient to any higher supernatural power which controls his destinies and which arbitrarily rewards and punishes. [Buddhism] does not condemn any other religion. But Buddhism recognizes the infinite latent possibilities of man and teaches that man can gain deliverance from suffering by his own efforts. . . . Buddhism cannot, therefore, strictly be called a religion because it is [not] a system of faith and worship.[25]

## Important Buddhist Writings

Another key difference between Buddhism and more conventional faiths relates to sacred literature. The Buddhists have no single, sacred, highly revered text like the Jewish Torah, Christian Bible, or Muslim Koran. Nevertheless, Buddhism does have some widely respected texts, written after the Buddha's death, that contain some of the faith's core beliefs.

These manuscripts were initially written in several languages, including Pali, Sanskrit, Tibetan, and Chinese. Over the centuries Buddhists in various parts of Asia divided the texts into two general categories. The first contains large numbers of sutras,

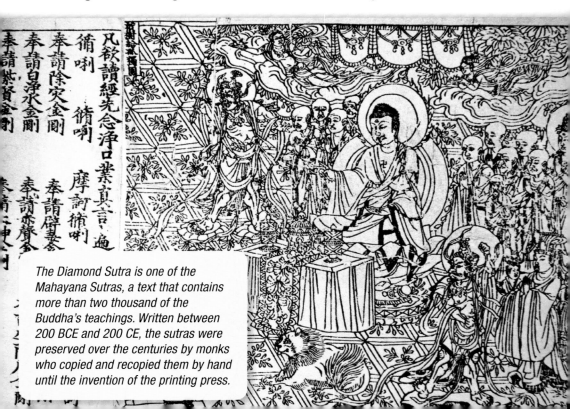

The Diamond Sutra is one of the Mahayana Sutras, a text that contains more than two thousand of the Buddha's teachings. Written between 200 BCE and 200 CE, the sutras were preserved over the centuries by monks who copied and recopied them by hand until the invention of the printing press.

Although the Buddha was not a political figure and supported no specific political system, the belief system he founded is essentially democratic in character. This is the conclusion of the leading Buddhist figure in the modern world, Tibet's Dalai Lama. In this excerpt from one of his many writings, he explains why this is the case.

> The Buddha made it clear that his followers were not to take even what he said at face value, but were to examine and test it as a goldsmith tests the quality of gold. But if we are prevented from using our discrimination and creativity, we lose one of the basic characteristics of a human being. Therefore, the political, social and cultural freedom that democracy entails is of immense value and importance. No system of government is perfect, but democracy is closest to our essential human nature. It is also the only stable foundation upon which a just and free global political structure can be built. So it is in all our interests that those of us who already enjoy democracy should actively support everybody's right to do so.

The Dalai Lama, "Buddhism and Democracy," His Holiness the 14th Dalai Lama of Tibet, 1993. www.dalai lama.com.

passages believed to be the preserved words of the Buddha himself. The other category of texts is made up of secondary materials, including histories of the Buddha, his followers, and Buddhist movements; commentaries penned by monks, scholars, and other respected Buddhists; and quotes by respected Buddhist teachers.

Some important Buddhist writings are cherished by and quoted from more often by members of certain sects of the faith as opposed to members of other sects. The Tripitaka, translated literally as "three baskets," is a well-known example. This earliest Buddhist writing, dating to the four centuries immediately following the Buddha's passing, is particularly revered by Theravada Buddhists. It has three principal sections. The first contains rules and advice for devout Buddhist monks; the second consists of more than ten thousand sutras attributed to the Buddha and some of his initial disciples; and the third is made up of a long summary of the Buddha's teachings.

The Tripitaka is also held dear by Mahayana Buddhists. However, they consider another early writing equally important. Most often called the Mahayana Sutras, it was written between 200 BCE and 200 CE and contains more than two thousand of the Buddha's sayings. Another well-regarded Buddhist text is the Bardo Thodol Chenmo, or Tibetan Book of the Dead. Thought to have been written in the eighth century CE by a Tibetan monk, it puts into words the thoughts that a number of people have supposedly had just before their deaths.

These and other traditional Buddhist writings still exist, thanks to the hard work of many generations of monks dwelling in monasteries across Asia. They carefully copied and recopied the manuscripts by hand, until printing presses were introduced in early modern times. These individuals were motivated by Buddhist beliefs and dedicated their entire lives to making those principles available to all future generations.

# CHAPTER FOUR

# How Do Buddhists Practice Their Faith?

Buddhist customs, practices, and rituals help adherents bring their beliefs and spiritual feelings to life. Certain practices have been a part of the faith since the Buddha's time. Thereafter, each new generation embraced and perpetuated them, as well as occasionally adding new customs and rituals.

As a result, modern Buddhist practices are numerous, extremely varied, and culturally rich. The most time-consuming, elaborate, and demanding one is becoming a monk and spending one's life in a monastery. Only a small percentage of Buddhists take that path. Most members of the faith immerse themselves in a number of simpler but regular social and spiritual practices. These include daily meditation, prayer, and chanting; adopting a special diet; taking part in holiday festivals; and observance of traditional marriage and funeral customs.

These and other practices are thought on the one hand to pay homage to the Buddha. On the other, they make all Buddhists feel like they are part of something bigger than themselves—a greater community. According to Gil Fronsdal of the Insight Meditation Center in Redwood City, California, various Buddhist practices "help create community and mutual support." They "can be as ordinary as greeting people with a handshake and as extraordinary as an elaborate memorial ceremony that brings healing to grief."[26]

## Monks and the Sangha

Usually the *most* elaborate Buddhist ceremonies are the ones that take place in and around monasteries. These institutions are populated mostly by monks who have devoted their lives to living out Buddhist ideas and principles. In some Buddhist sects,

Buddhist monks receive alms from villagers in modern-day Myanmar. In this way they follow the practices of the earliest monks, who traveled from village to village begging for food and sharing their beliefs with anyone interested in learning about them.

women take on this role, but this is uncommon. Considered as a whole, the monasteries and their residents make up the *sangha*.

During the Buddha's lifetime no monasteries yet existed. The faith's monastic movement began shortly after his death. From that time on, certain rules and practices for monks were established. They had to shave their heads and wear simple robes, for example. Most of these practices remain in place today. Modern monks are expected not to lie, drink alcoholic beverages, sleep on raised beds (that is, beds with innersprings or extra padding), eat a meal after noontime, or accept money for their work.

One of the key tasks of Buddhist monks was and remains setting a good example of piety and morality for ordinary Buddhists to follow. Also by tradition, the monks teach the faith's beliefs to any non-Buddhists who want to learn them. The Buddha told his initial followers to teach "for the welfare of the many, out of compassion for the world."[27] The monks still carry on that ideal. They never use force of any kind to spread the faith. When possible, they follow the example of the earliest Buddhist monks, described here by an authority on religion:

Early Buddhist evangelism [missionary work] usually consisted of a pair of monks entering a village, going from house to house with their begging bowls until they had enough for the one meal they ate each day. The monks would then return to the outskirts of the town, where they would often be followed by [villagers who] wished to talk with them. The monks would share what they knew, then move on to the next village.[28]

## Meditation and Chanting

As examples for others to follow, the monks who make up the *sangha* regularly engage in certain practices that have become standard not only for them but also for the vast majority of Buddhists. Perhaps chief among these practices is meditation. As Buddhists do it, meditation is a form of mental concentration intended to clear the mind of everyday thoughts and focus on a specific task. Ultimately, or at least in theory, that task is to become enlightened, as the Buddha did.

In a more practical sense, however, Buddhists who practice daily meditation usually do so for less lofty reasons. The goal might be to enjoy some momentary rest from one's normal routines, to find inner peace, or to gain new insights about some problem or other aspect of life. Whatever their immediate goals for meditating may be, many say it makes them calmer and happier in their everyday life. According to the Buddha Dharma Education Association, "Meditation is now accepted as having a highly therapeutic effect upon the mind and is used by many professional mental health workers to help induce relaxation, overcome phobias, and bring about self-awareness. The Buddha's insights into the human mind are helping people as much today as they did in ancient times."[29]

> *"The Buddha's insights into the human mind are helping people as much today as they did in ancient times."*[29]
>
> —Buddha Dharma Education Association

# Mantras Harmonize Body and Mind

A widely respected teacher of Tibetan Buddhism, Alexander Berzin, explains what mantras are and their several possible uses.

The Sanskrit word *mantra* is made up of its root, *man*, meaning "mind," with the suffix -*tra* meaning "tool," precisely describing the kind of "mind-tool" that mantras are in Buddhism. They are also found in all Indian spiritual traditions, and beyond as well. The Tibetans, for example, understood them as a form of "mind-protection," a tool to protect the mind from disturbing thoughts and emotions. Recited vocally or mentally, in or out of meditation, mantras help our minds to settle down. . . .

There are a wide range of applications for mantra practice in Buddhism. As a start, they regulate the breath and subtle energies, allowing our minds to calm down. They then help us to stay focused on positive states of minds or emotions, like love and compassion. Furthermore, they help integrate and harmonize our body, speech and mind. Finally, through deeper practice, mantras help us to gain access to the subtlest level of mind, [leading] us to the actual attainment of enlightenment for the benefit of all.

Alexander Berzin, "What Is a Mantra?," Study Buddhism. https://studybuddhism.com.

It is fairly common among Buddhists, especially those in Southeast Asia, to employ chanting along with and sometimes separately from meditation. In India in the era in which the Buddha lived, few people could read or write. So a monk, scribe, or some other person who wanted to pass on a story or important information to someone else chanted it. The listener steadily memorized it and perhaps later chanted it to a third person.

As time went on, Buddhists transformed chanting into more of a personal ritual, often involving continually repeating the same set of words or phrases. Many who do it claim it helps take their minds off mundane daily events and focus more on a specific thought or idea. In some places chanting is also performed as a public ritual during important life events, such as birth celebrations, marriage ceremonies, and funerals.

## Mantras and Prayers

Another practice directly connected to chanting and meditation is the use of mantras. These are special sounds that many Buddhists think of as an added tool for maintaining a state of concentration. According to noted American Buddhist teacher Alexander Berzin, mantras allow "our minds to calm down. They then help us to stay focused on positive states of minds or emotions, like love." He points out that in the modern world sometimes "political parties and commercial brands promote their 'mantras' to us in the form of catchy slogans. None of this, however, is their intended use in Buddhist practice. In Buddhism, mantras are utilized as sophisticated tools to help us to generate and stay focused on beneficial states of mind, like compassion for others, or clarity of thought."[30]

Mantras are particularly popular among the followers of Tibetan Buddhism. Their best-known mantra is also the most renowned of all Buddhist mantras. Consisting of the syllables *om*, *mani*, *padme*, and *hum*, it has no specific definition in and of itself. Rather, each syllable has a meaning of its own, and chanted together (over and over) the sounds add up to a potentially potent aid to meditation.

Many Buddhists own and use strings of beads called *malas*, with which they count the number of mantras they have recited in a single session. The fact that *malas* are informally called "prayer beads" is revealing. Buddhists often define mantras as prayers. Praying is not the same in Buddhism as it is in Judaism, Christianity, and Islam, in which a person prays to a divine being to ask for something.

> "[Mantras] help us to generate and stay focused on beneficial states of mind, like compassion for others."[30]
>
> —American Buddhist teacher Alexander Berzin

In Buddhism, by contrast, a prayer is a form of meditation that is thought to send out good signals, or vibrations, that are

**43**

felt within the person praying and, it is hoped, within society as a whole. Some Buddhists pray to the Buddha, but not to ask him for something. Rather, they invoke his positive image and make vows, or promises, in his name that they will do good things. A minority of Buddhists think that deceased Buddhas, or people who have achieved total enlightenment, *do* hear their vows. But most members of the faith would agree that saying a prayer is like sending a greeting card to the universe and hoping that its positive vibrations have a beneficial effect. A leading practitioner of Tibetan Buddhism, Sarah Harding, suggests that prayer

> can be seen as an aspiration, as setting your mind in a certain direction. Whether you have a particular other being or other power in mind is not necessarily the main thrust of it; the main point is that you are putting your mind in that direction. For instance, if you send a Christmas card that says, "May there be peace on earth," you are not necessarily asking someone to bestow [that peace].[31]

Instead, she explains, one simply hopes that his or her positive thoughts will help make it come to pass.

## Diets, Holidays, and Pilgrimages

Meditating, chanting, and praying are all practices that Buddhists believe can aid one's mental processes. To improve their physical well-being, many Buddhists engage in special dietary practices. The most common one by far is vegetarianism—essentially, refraining from eating meat. Not all Buddhists are vegetarians. Indeed, numerous modern Buddhist monasteries serve meat. In part, this is because the Buddha himself never forbade meat eating. A major reason (though not the only one) why many Buddhists choose to be vegetarians is moral in nature. They see the killing of animals specifically to consume their flesh as unethical. Ultimately, most Buddhist teachings say that the choice to either eat or not eat meat lies with the individual.

Another practice that is optional for Buddhists is taking part in the celebrations associated with the faith's various annual holidays. Some of these ceremonial days differ from one Buddhist sect to another. But a few are more or less universal among all

South Koreans celebrate the Buddha's birthday in 2016. Such celebrations often feature paper lanterns, which are thought to symbolize good fortune.

practitioners. The largest in many Asian nations is the new year. Some Buddhists observe it on December 31 or January 1 like people in most of the rest of the world. A minority of Buddhists celebrate the new year when January's first full moon arrives—most often in mid-January. During the week leading up to the big day, people often clean their houses thoroughly, pay some or all of their debts, and prepare and eat special foods. Although these foods vary somewhat from region to region, popular throughout southern Asia is cooked rice sprinkled with ground jasmine flowers. Another widely liked dish consists of a mixture of banana, black beans, and coconut- or mango-flavored rice, all wrapped in banana leaves.

Globally, however, the faith's biggest holiday is the Buddha's birthday. Buddhists in different lands sometimes observe it on

One thought-provoking question sometimes arises when a Buddhist dies and undergoes cremation. Namely, will he or she return in another form? A minority of Buddhists believe that even after a person has been cremated, his or her essence, or soul, may survive and be reborn in another body. However, most Buddhist sects neither accept nor teach this principle, most often called reincarnation. In mainstream Buddhist thought, no soul exists to survive death, so there is no reincarnation. However, most Buddhists do propose that the negative or positive energy that someone emits in his or her lifetime can survive in a roundabout way. That energy can affect—in either bad ways or good ways—the world in which future generations grow up. Buddhists call the force of this invisible energy karma. Karma, according to Buddhist teachings, consists simply of the actions and reactions of human-generated energy floating through the natural environment.

different days and with different traditions. In some temples, for example, the monks celebrate by preparing special vegetarian meals for any and all visitors. In a number of Buddhist communities, meanwhile, the faithful engage in charitable acts. Some donate money or goods to the poor; others buy animals from slaughterhouses and either release them or keep them as pets; and in some Asian countries, Buddhist temples and homes display paper lanterns shaped like flowers. Use of the lanterns dates back to ancient times and is thought to symbolize good fortune.

Another way that some Buddhists honor the Buddha's memory is by going on pilgrimages, or spiritual journeys. Pilgrimage sites for Buddhists exist throughout Asia. One popular one is Putuo Shan, an island off China's coast, which features some important temples. Japan also has several widely admired ancient temples that Buddhists enjoy visiting. At such a place, pilgrims typically meditate for a while in quiet spots. Yet like tourists everywhere, they also take many photos and collect souvenirs when available.

## Localized Practices

Holiday celebrations and pilgrimages are group practices shared by most members of the larger Buddhist community. Other practices and ceremonies are more localized and revolve around individuals and families. One of the more prominent examples consists of marriage traditions and rites.

In Buddhism, getting married is regarded neither as holy nor unholy. That is, the faith does not consider marriage to be a religious matter, and there is no time-honored tradition of staging weddings in temples in the way that many Christians get married in churches. Nevertheless, Buddhist couples *can* wed in temples if they want; and brides and grooms do often ask monks to bless their unions after the fact. Because monks set an example for

Like some other practices, funeral customs vary among different Buddhist communities. Here, an altar adorned with flowers honors the deceased in this photograph from modern-day Cambodia.

others, their approval is thought to bring good luck to a marriage. The marriage ceremony can differ somewhat from one country or Buddhist sect to another. But in the most common version, the bride, the groom, and their guests stand before an image of the Buddha that is festooned with flowers. The couple lights some candles and may recite some phrases from an ancient Buddhist text. Then they turn to the guests, and the groom says, "Towards my wife I undertake to love and respect her, be kind and considerate, be faithful, [and] provide gifts to please her." Next, the bride states, "Towards my husband I undertake to perform my household duties efficiently, be hospitable to my in-laws and friends of my husband, be faithful, [and] discharge my responsibilities lovingly and conscientiously."[32] After the ceremony, as in most non-Buddhist weddings, everyone engages in feasting, singing, and dancing.

> *"Towards my wife I undertake to love and respect her, be kind and considerate, be faithful."*[32]
>
> —Part of a Buddhist groom's traditional wedding vow

Among other localized Buddhist practices are funeral customs. Ceremonies surrounding death and funerals are extremely diverse among the world's numerous Buddhist communities. However, a few general rules and customs hold true for most members of the faith. For instance, in most Buddhist communities, embalming a body is frowned on. With a few exceptions, a majority of Buddhists choose to be cremated, mostly because the Buddha made that choice for himself.

The funeral services usually include customs such as chanting or singing some of the Buddha's teachings, offering flowers and fruit to the deceased's family, burning incense, and ringing bells or gongs or playing other musical instruments. As an expert on such services points out, those in attendance should consider "performing good deeds on behalf of the deceased person." He adds, "All attendees should be sending good thoughts to the family and contemplating the impermanence of life."[33] As is true of most Buddhist practices, those surrounding death tend to celebrate the specialness of each individual human life.

# CHAPTER FIVE

# Buddhist Architecture, Sculpture, and Painting

Over the centuries, Buddhism has exerted a spiritual and intellectual influence over countless people in more than a hundred countries. All told, billions converted to or were raised in the faith, which deeply affected the way they saw themselves, their societies, and the world as a whole. In no less profound a manner, people around the globe—especially in Asia—felt, and continue to feel, the cultural influence of Buddhist-inspired arts.

The international artistic disciplines of architecture, sculpture, and painting have especially been shaped to one degree or another by Buddhist models. The proof lies partly in museums in all the world's major cities. There, entire wings are devoted to Buddhist-inspired artistic masterpieces. Also, Buddhist temples, shrines, and monasteries—in a very real way composing living museums—adorn the vast landscape of Southeast Asia.

## The Rise of the Stupa

The architecture of these often stunning structures was among the first of the artistic areas to be affected by the early rise of Buddhism in India. Shortly after the Buddha's passing in the early 400s BCE, his followers wanted to erect shrines in which to store relics associated with him. As Baruch College art historian Karen Shelby explains, "Relics are objects associated with an esteemed person, including that person's bones (or ashes in the case of the Buddha), or things the person used or had worn. The veneration, or respect, for relics is prevalent in many religious faiths, particularly in Christianity."[34]

In addition to protecting the Buddha's ashes, clothes, and other similar relics, his followers envisioned that the new shrines would be focal points for learning about and perpetuating his enlightened ideas. They searched for a sturdy but attractive shape for these structures and quickly settled on the stupa. This basic architectural form had already been used in India for several centuries. In Sanskrit, the word *stupa* means "heaped" or "piled up," which is why early Indians chose it to describe burial mounds, including those containing the remains of rulers.

The first stupas were simply mounds of earth with tombs inside them. But over time, they evolved into more elaborate and more strongly built structures. When early Buddhists adopted them, they stacked stone blocks or fired bricks in circular fashion, creating a dome, with its thickest portion at ground level. Buddhist stupas—the largest used as temples—came to be plastered, painted, and embellished with statues, carvings, and other decorations.

One of the finest examples of these early Buddhist buildings is the so-called Mahastupa, or Great Stupa, at Sanchi in north-central India. Its imposing dome is 120 feet (36.6 m) across and 54 feet (16.5 m) high. Architectural expert Francis D.K. Ching describes it as "a solid mass built up in the form of hundreds of stone rings [each composed of individual stone blocks] that were surfaced with plaster and painted."[35]

## Impressive Local Adaptations

As time went on, this pleasing architectural style spread, along with Buddhist ideas and beliefs, to neighboring lands. Buddhist stupas were erected by the thousands in Burma (now called Myanmar), Sri Lanka, China, Cambodia, Korea, Thailand, and Japan. Leading trademarks of the faith, they continued to evolve and took on distinctive local features in each of these lands.

An impressive example of these unique adaptations of the stupa form is the Shwezigon Pagoda, constructed in Burma in 1102. A pagoda is a tower having a number of separate layers stacked atop one another. Builders in Burma and some other regions opted to place the stupa at the summit of such a stack, thereby creating a pagoda-style temple. At Shwezigon, the stupa is covered with gold leaf and perches atop five beautifully ornamented layers, each with a separate outer walkway. Overall, the huge temple is 160 feet (49 m) high and the same distance across at the base. As is the case with other Buddhist temples, monks regularly conduct rituals inside, while ordinary Buddhists meditate both inside and outside the building's grounds.

A different sort of pagoda-style Buddhist temple developed in Japan. In the Japanese version, in each tier the eaves, or overhanging roof edges, stick outward several feet. In addition, the eaves' tips curve upward a bit, imparting an uplifting, graceful appearance to the structure as a whole. An excellent example is the five-tiered pagoda that stands in the large-scale Horyu-ji temple

Early Buddhists constructed thousands of stupas, domed structures intended to be used as tombs, temples, and centers of learning. Pictured is the Great Stupa located at Sanchi in north-central India.

complex at Nara, Japan. The pagoda soars 115 feet (35 m) into the air. The first floor features some fifty sculpted figures depicting scenes from the Buddha's life.

## Changing Influences

The Horyu-ji figures at Nara are an example of a later, mature style of Buddhist sculpture. Many centuries before, ancient Greek sculptors had influenced early Buddhist sculptors in certain ways. Buddhist artisans had then absorbed those ideas and over time had developed their own versions. This eventually led to a distinctly Buddhist approach that subsequently had an enormous influence on Asian sculpture in general, including the Nara figures.

This chain of events can best be seen in the familiar carved figures that depict the Buddha himself. Images of his face and body were not always accepted or done. In the faith's first few centuries, it was viewed as disrespectful to fashion statues that showed his specific facial and other features. This is now referred to as the aniconic phase of Buddhist sculpture. Artists devoted their skills instead to creating objects indirectly associated with the Buddha. For instance, they often carved the Buddhist wheel of law, which showed symbols that stood for several of the Buddha's key teachings. Also common were sculptures of the special tree he sat under when he achieved enlightenment and footprints suggestive of his walking long distances to preach his ideas.

By the first century CE, with the start of the iconic phase of Buddhist sculpture, however, it was no longer seen as disrespectful to carve images of the Buddha. This was largely thanks to the influence of Indo-Greek artists. They hailed from the small Greek kingdoms established in and near western India in the third and second centuries BCE. Many of the residents of those nations converted to Buddhism, and the arts they produced later came to be labeled Greco-Buddhist. This is because they combined early Buddhist themes and concepts with Greek ones.

One important traditional sculptural practice long employed in Greece was to create highly realistic statues, figurines, and busts of gods and mythical heroes. Indo-Greek artists carried on that practice and applied it in their own works, including those with Buddhist themes. In this way they became the first sculptors to

Besides the temples or shrines erected in the shape of a stupa, another important early Buddhist architectural type was the monastery, or *vihara*. Usually, such a structure, at first made of wood and later bricks, had living quarters for the monks clustered around a central assembly hall called a *chaitya*. In some of these halls, the monks built small indoor stupas. This feature became especially prominent in the Buddhist monasteries that were cut into cliffs in central India, including the large caves at Ajanta and Bhaja. In the words of Baruch College art historian Karen Shelby:

> The main *chaitya* hall . . . at Bhaja contains a solid stone *stupa* in the nave flanked by two side aisles. It is the earliest example of this type of rock-cut cave. . . . Eventually, the rock-cut monasteries became quite complex. They consisted of several stories with inner courtyards and veranda. Some facades had reliefs, images projecting from the stone, of the Buddha. . . . A *stupa* was still placed in the central hall, but now an image of the Buddha was carved into it, underscoring that the Buddha is the *stupa*. Stories from the Buddha's life were also, at times, added to the interior in both paintings and reliefs.

Karen Shelby, "Buddhist Monasteries," Khan Academy, 2017. www.khanacademy.org.

carve statues that explicitly portrayed the Buddha in human form. Usually, they depicted him with wavy hair. It also became common to show him wearing sandals and a cloak similar to the toga-like Greek garment known as a himation.

As Buddhism eventually spread well beyond India, other Asian peoples approved of and adopted that Greek approach to sculpting the Buddha. In a way this was ironic; that is, it eagerly embraced a custom that contradicted one of the most basic Buddhist teachings. The Buddha had emphasized that he was a man, not a god. Yet in carving him, the Indo-Greek sculptors fell back on a tradition of portraying exceptional humans in god-like form. About that image of the Buddha as a man-god, art historian Peter Holleran writes that it "was essentially inspired by

Greek mythological culture. This iconic art was characterized by a 'realistic idealism,' combining realistic human features, proportions, attitudes, and attributes, together with a sense of perfection and serenity reaching to the divine. This expression of the Buddha as both a man and a god became the [visual] model for subsequent Buddhist art."[36]

## China's and Japan's Giant Buddhas

Indeed, as time went on peoples across Southeast Asia created countless godlike statues of the Buddha, some smaller than a person's hand, others towering to more than 100 feet (30 m). In

The Leshan Giant Buddha was carved from the side of a cliff near the Chinese city of Leshan. The structure is the world's biggest sculpted image of Buddha as well as the world's largest premodern statue.

some regions, these figures became the dominant forms of Buddhist sculpture. For instance, nearly every carved image made in Thailand in the early centuries CE was a statue of the Buddha.

In China, Korea, Japan, and other parts of Asia, in contrast, Buddhist sculpture was important but not dominant and was far more diverse in style. In these lands Buddhist artistic themes tended to combine with and complement local traditional ones. In China, for example, sculptors had long employed wood, metal, and terra-cotta (baked clay) in their work. After Buddhism took hold there, these materials remained standard; and slowly but surely a growing number of sculptors used them to reflect and promote Buddhist beliefs and themes. This trend reached its zenith of technical skill, artistic realism, and sheer beauty during the T'ang Dynasty (ca. 618–907 CE).

> *"This expression of the Buddha as both a man and a god became the [visual] model for subsequent Buddhist art."* [36]
>
> —Art historian Peter Holleran

Several of those magnificent works have survived intact or nearly so. Perhaps the most striking is the Leshan Giant Buddha, carved from the side of a cliff near the city of Leshan in south-central China. The statue towers to a height of 233 feet (71 m). It is not only the world's biggest sculpted image of Buddha, but also by far the planet's largest premodern statue. Dozens of other large-scale statues of the Buddha still dot China's landscape.

Ancient and medieval Japanese sculptors were also greatly inspired by Buddhist beliefs and themes. Before Buddhism arrived in Japan, most sculptures were small figures of people, animals, and houses made of terra-cotta. Called *haniwa* in Japanese, people traditionally laid them at the entrances of tombs in the hope that they would protect the bodies lying within.

After Buddhist teachings spread across Japan, local sculptors started both carving and casting images of the faith's famous founder. Some, like many in China, were enormous. In 752 CE, the Japanese emperor Shomu sponsored the creation at Nara of a bronze statue of the Buddha measuring 52 feet (16 m) tall. "This colossal Buddha," says Temple University scholar Deanna MacDonald, "required all the available copper in Japan and workers

Noted English art critic Jonathan Glancey has closely studied the famous paintings in the Ajanta caves in west-central India. He points out that in 1999, archaeologists began a long-term examination and restoration of these magnificent works. This project, Glancey writes, has

> revealed the intense colours and sheer beauty of many of the 1st Century AD portraits along with the subtlety of their artists' use of perspective, shading and other three-dimensional techniques including the use of bright stones, notably lapis lazuli from Afghanistan.
>
> Their meticulous restoration raised anew questions asked many times over the past 200 years. How did the artists paint so well, with such precise use of colour, in the dark recesses of these rock-carved prayer halls and monasteries? Just how many architects, masons, sculptors and painters would have been at work between from circa AD 460–500 when so much of this glorious place . . . was created? . . .
>
> The many archaeological ventures over the past two centuries seeking to answer these questions, as well as to uncover, document and conserve this feast of Buddhist creativity have added immeasurably to Ajanta's fame.

Jonathan Glancey, "The Ajanta Caves: Discovering Lost Treasure," BBC, February 23, 2015. www.bbc.com.

used an estimated 163,000 cubic feet of charcoal to produce the metal alloy and form the bronze figure."[37]

Three centuries later the awesome Nara Buddha and the temple in which it sat were demolished in a civil war. "The destruction of this revered temple shocked Japan," MacDonald points out. When the conflict ended, reconstruction immediately began. "The aristocracy and the warrior elite contributed funds" and casting the giant bronze Buddha "again became the largest building project in Japan."[38] That replacement still stands inside Nara's stunning temple complex, which was named a World Heritage Site by the United Nations Educational, Scientific and Cultural Organization in 1998.

## Buddhism-Inspired Painting

Along with architecture and sculpture, ancient Asian painting was highly influenced by the spread of Buddhism. Different painting traditions, each using distinctive techniques, were affected. In India and some other areas, one of the most prevalent was the fresco method, in which an artist applies paint to a layer of plaster before the plaster completely dries. The paint and plaster intermingle and become inseparable. This means that the paint will not later rub off and stays brighter longer.

An outstanding example of Buddhist fresco painting consists of thousands of images on the walls of some large caves at Ajanta in west-central India. Created in the first few centuries CE, these superlative works rival the famous frescos crafted during Europe's Renaissance a millennium later. Many of the Ajanta paintings depict the Buddha in well-known scenes from his life.

> *"The destruction of [the] revered [Nara] temple shocked Japan."*[38]
>
> —Scholar Deanna MacDonald

In Ajanta's *Court Life Scene*, for example, young Prince Siddhartha, the future Buddha, climbs onto his wife's bed to tell her he has decided to become a monk. Both figures, art historian Enrico Annosica explains,

> are depicted with great vigor. The woman, wearing a dress of fine material, leans delicately against the body of her husband. Her attitude suggests confidence in her powers of seduction. [Siddhartha's] body is athletic and firmly structured. Rich [decoration] indicates the rank of the prince and reminds us of the luxurious worldly pleasures that he will now have the strength to leave behind.[39]

A different painting tradition developed in China and Japan. There, many artists first made ink outlines and sometimes filled them in with colors, mostly light pastels. Other times they employed a range of light and darker grays, a technique known as monochrome.

Buddhist ink paintings began to come into their own in China in the 600s CE, and in the centuries that followed, a number of great masters were widely copied. They included Wang Wei (born 699), Jing Hao (born ca. 870), and Fan Kuan (born ca. 960). Landscapes often depicted delicate renditions of bamboo stalks and country houses nestled near bamboo trees with graceful birds perched in their branches. These were popular in part because in ancient China bamboo was seen as a symbol of virtue and traditional values.

The influence of these painters was strong on Japanese, Tibetan, and other Asian artists beginning in the 700s CE. In Japan, Buddhism-inspired landscapes often expressed feelings like "melancholy [sadness], loneliness, naturalness, and age," says a Metropolitan Museum of Art expert. In this style, "a misshapen, worn peasant's jar is considered more beautiful than a pristine, carefully crafted dish. While the latter pleases the senses, the former stimulates the mind and emotions to contemplate the essence of reality. This artistic sensibility has had an enormous impact on Japanese culture up to modern times."[40] Indeed, ancient Buddhist arts still fill museums around the globe and continue to influence architects, sculptors, painters, and other artists in each new generation.

# CHAPTER SIX

# What Challenges Does Buddhism Face in the Modern World?

Like the world's other major faiths, Buddhism has faced, and continues to face, challenges in the modern world. Modern religious groups encounter two general kinds of dilemmas. Some are internal—that is, those that arise from within the ranks of the faithful; others are external, those imposed on the faith by outsiders.

Modern Buddhism's difficulties have been both internal and external in nature. Some have been around for a long time and have been the focus of much attention among the faith's adherents. Meanwhile, other more current challenges continue to crop up from time to time, often dictated by changing global political and social events.

In 2010 Buddhist Jeff Wilson, a professor of religion at Canada's University of Waterloo, was asked to speculate on the difficulties his faith could expect to deal with in the near future. He answered in part, "The relationship of Tibet and China is likely to remain a source of perpetual friction, with China unable to convert Tibet into a fully Chinese province and Tibet unable to pull itself out of China's influence."[41] This prediction proved correct, as since it was made, China and Tibet have remained at odds and displayed a marked inability to solve their differences.

Another challenge Buddhism may face, Wilson says, is "the ambition of global Christianity." He explains that some of the Christian churches in the West and in Asia have a strong desire to convert Asian Buddhists to Christianity. In the 1990s, for instance, evangelical Christian groups sent people to Cambodia in hopes of gaining converts. "Well-funded efforts to Christianize Asian cultures will continue to erode Buddhism's traditional heartlands,"[42] Wilson contended. Evangelical groups have continued to send missionaries to Cambodia and elsewhere to spread Christian beliefs.

## Dawn of the Twentieth Century

The challenges Wilson speaks of may well prove increasingly troublesome to Buddhism in the next few decades. In the meantime, however, Buddhism is still trying to deal with major challenges that have threatened the very fabric of the faith since the start of the twentieth century. The first one, which is internal in nature, consists of various degrees of disunity within Buddhism's ranks.

*"Well-funded efforts to Christianize Asian cultures will continue to erode Buddhism's traditional heartlands."[42]*

—Buddhist scholar Jeff Wilson

For many centuries Buddhism was divided into numerous individual sects, each with some distinct points of view and customs. These differing factions within the faith still existed at the start the twentieth century. By far the largest were three that had developed in ancient times. The Theravada remained the most conservative and continued to follow the earliest Buddhist beliefs and rituals. After the passage of more than two millennia, they still saw the Tripitaka as the most revered Buddhist text. The Theravada also tended to hold in the highest esteem individuals who chose to withdraw from the world to meditate and seek enlightenment. Monks therefore became especially respected—even viewed as superior humans—in Theravada Buddhism.

Meanwhile, in 1900 the Mahayana were still Buddhism's other major subdivision. By the advent of the modern era, the Mahayana had subdivided into several smaller branches, chief among them Zen Buddhists, Pure Land Buddhists, and Nicherin Buddhists. The differences between these groups were relatively small. All continued to view the Mahayana Sutras as equal in stature to the Tripitaka. In addition, the Mahayana had developed considerably more rituals and celebrations than the Theravada had.

A Christian church floats on a river in Cambodia. In the 1990s, evangelical Christian groups from the West sent people to the country in hopes of gaining converts among the Buddhist population.

The third major division of Buddhism that greeted the dawn of the twentieth century was Tibetan Buddhism. People sometimes call it Lamaism because its most respected and influential monks are referred to as lamas. The leading lama—seen as particularly admirable and high ranking—bears the title of Dalai Lama.

The beliefs and customs of Tibetan Buddhism are similar in some ways to those of Mahayana Buddhism. This is because they were originally one and the same sect, and the Tibetan version broke away from the Mahayana version in the 700s and 800s CE. The Tibetan school of Buddhism does contain several distinctive customs. In particular, it features some mystical elements that are unusual compared to the mainstream of Buddhists beliefs. These elements include belief in reincarnation; belief in supernatural beings or spirits, some good, others evil; the idea that these spirits can affect earthly life; and the idea that certain magical formulas can keep evil beings at bay.

## Striving for Unity

In the early 1900s, facing an increasingly modernized and politically divisive world, leaders of these major Buddhist sects became more and more apprehensive. For centuries most Buddhists had stayed out of politics and wars in their native countries. But from the late 1800s on, local governments in Japan and other parts of Asia saw this as a weakness and treated Buddhists with contempt.

In the decades that followed, a growing number of Buddhist thinkers argued that most or all Buddhists should avoid potential persecution by uniting. That goal of unity at first proved difficult to realize. This may have been due in part to the political and social chaos caused by World War I (1914–1918), World War II (1939–1945), and other conflicts in the early twentieth century.

Leading Buddhists finally managed to achieve some degree of unity in 1950. That year, in Colombo, Sri Lanka, they established the World Fellowship of Buddhists (WFB). The 129 delegates from twenty-seven nations, representing all Buddhist sects, agreed on a number of shared goals. One was to try to maintain unity among all Buddhists. Another was to promote basic Buddhist ideals that all agreed on. Still another objective, according to the organization's charter, was "to organize and carry on activities in the field of social, educational, cultural, and other humanitarian services." In so doing, it was essential to treat "members of all the sects as brothers, and [to perform] beneficial and charitable acts for both Buddhists and non-Buddhists."[43] Today the WFB has offices in thirty-five countries.

## A Government and Faith in Exile

The WFB and some other similar global Buddhist organizations that formed later have at least partially overcome the challenge of disunity among the diverse Buddhist sects. However, whatever unity *has* been achieved has often been blunted by the strong pacifist stance that all Buddhists agree is central to their faith. A number of external forces have taken advantage of that refusal to fight back by persecuting Buddhists. This external threat continues to be the biggest single challenge facing modern Buddhism.

Although outbursts of political repression and violence against Buddhists occurred on and off during the twentieth century, all

# Buddhist Unity Plus World Peace

After the emergence of the WFB in 1950, other organizations formed to promote unity among Buddhists. One of these groups, the World Buddhist Sangha Council (WBSC), was founded in 1966 in Sri Lanka. Its members belong to all three major Buddhist sects. Among the WBSC's stated goals is to enhance harmony among different Buddhist traditions. Another is "propagating the Buddha's teaching of compassion to promote world peace." The WBSC also sponsors specialized teachers whose job is to educate non-Buddhists about Buddhist beliefs and practices.

Still another unified Buddhist organization, the International Buddhist Confederation (IBC), formed in India in 2013. Like the WFB and WBSC, the newer group emphasizes not only Buddhist unity but also global peace. At the IBC's first meeting, its leader stressed that Buddhism has always promoted choosing peace over war. "If we really and truly want peace, compassion and love for each other, and respect for each other in this very diverse world," she said, "there can be no better teaching than the teachings of Lord Buddha."

World Buddhist Sangha Council, "Constitution." www.wbsc886.org.

Quoted in Press Trust of India, "First International Buddhist Confederation Held in Delhi," *Business Standard* (New Delhi, India), September 9, 2013. www.business-standard.com.

paled in comparison to the struggle of Tibetan Buddhists, which is ongoing. In 1959 Communist China seized control of its southern neighbor, Tibet. That included Tibet's government, headed by the Dalai Lama. In the two years that followed, the invaders proceeded to wantonly destroy more than six thousand Tibetan Buddhist monasteries. This was part of an organized attempt to eradicate the country's Buddhist heritage.

Approximately one hundred thousand Tibetan Buddhists saw no other choice but to flee their homeland. They put their full trust in their leader, the Dalai Lama. Born Tenzin Gyatso in 1935, he had undergone a major transformation as a child. The foremost Tibetan monks had examined him and concluded that he was no ordinary child, but rather the reincarnation of several earlier Dalai

The head of Tibet's government, the Dalai Lama (pictured) and thousands of his Buddhist followers were forced to flee the country in 1959 when Communist China seized control. They established a government in exile in India and have ever since sought to peacefully regain their country and reunite with their fellow Tibetans.

Lamas. In this way he became the nation's leading spiritual figure and later, in 1950, its political leader as well.

After their escape from Tibet, the Dalai Lama and his followers established a Tibetan government in exile in Dharamsala, India. Ever since, they have fought to get their country back and to reunite with the Tibetans in their homeland. Because they are pacifists, that "fight" has taken the form of a vigorous, relentless, but always nonviolent media campaign. The Dalai Lama has consistently led these efforts. He received the Nobel Peace Prize in 1989. The Nobel committee cited his advocacy of peaceful solutions to working toward maintaining Tibet's cultural heritage in the face of Chinese aggression.

## Toward Tibetan Democracy

Still waging his campaign to regain Tibet and its Buddhist traditions, the Dalai Lama regularly publishes books and appears on television shows in countries around the globe. Clearly an intelligent, learned individual, he also displays a sharp sense of humor. This has done much to win the sympathies of many people for the plight of the Tibetan refugees.

Through his amiable personality and good works, the Dalai Lama has also succeeded in showing many non-Buddhists why Buddhism has attracted so many followers over the centuries. In fact, he argues, as a philosophy Buddhist thought has much in common with the freedom-loving ideals that instigated the founding of modern democracies like France, Britain, and the United States. Modern Buddhists, too, he explains, believe in pursuing lives of liberty and happiness. Also like modern democratic governments, he points out, Buddhists see all faiths as equal and promote freedom of religion. "I personally have great admiration for secular democracy," the Dalai Lama has stated. "Freedom is something to be shared and enjoyed in the company of others." He continues:

> **"I personally have great admiration for secular democracy."[44]**
>
> —The Dalai Lama

Although the Tibetans outside Tibet have been reduced to the status of refugees, we have the freedom to exercise our rights. Our brothers and sisters in Tibet, despite being in their own country, do not even have the right to life. Therefore, those of us in exile have had a responsibility to contemplate and plan for a future Tibet. Over the years we have tried through various means to achieve a model of true democracy.[44]

## From Abuses to Increasing Acceptance

Another overt attack on Buddhists happened in a different Asian nation beginning in 2007. In October of that year, in Myanmar (formerly Burma), the military generals in charge there cracked down on a group of Buddhist monks. The monks had been peacefully protesting a recent doubling of the price of gasoline. They were doing this on behalf of millions of impoverished Burmese, most

# Tibet as a Free Democracy?

The current Tibetan Dalai Lama lectures widely, in part to gain worldwide support for the Tibetan Buddhists in exile. He often argues that modern democracies should offer such support because the Tibetan exiles have done their best to adopt democratic principles. Indeed, he promises that if the exiles can regain control of their country, they will run it as a modern democracy. The Dalai Lama states that he looks forward

> to the time when we could devise a political system suited both to our traditions and to the demands of the modern world. A democracy that has non-violence and peace at its roots. We have recently embarked on changes that will further democratize and strengthen our administration in exile. For many reasons, I have decided that I will not be the head of . . . the government when Tibet becomes independent. The future head of the Tibetan Government must be someone popularly elected by the people. There are many advantages to such a step and it will enable us to become a true and complete democracy. I hope that these moves will allow the people of Tibet to have a clear say in determining the future of their country.

The Dalai Lama, "Buddhism and Democracy," His Holiness the 14th Dalai Lama of Tibet, 1993. www.dalai lama.com.

of them Buddhists, who simply could not afford to pay so much for fuel.

The generals could have simply ignored the protests. Instead, however, they decided to go after the monks, who everyone knew would not fight back. Soldiers beat and arrested thousands of the monks. More than thirty of the robed protesters were killed, and the government made matters even worse by closing down nearly all the country's monasteries. In an act that inspired widespread outrage, moreover, the generals ordered their troops to take over Burmese Buddhism's most revered site, the Shwedagon Temple.

Meanwhile, many of the monks who had been jailed endured various abuses. Frequently, dozens of them were pushed into a single small cell, so that no one was able to lie down. They had no toilets, were given only a handful of rice to eat each day, and were brutally beaten over and over again. Some of the monks were eventually released. But some others received long prison sentences. In a valiant stand, they refused to cease their

protests. One, thirty-year-old U Gambira, who was given a sentence of sixty-three years, told visitors from the international aid group Human Rights Watch, "We adhere to nonviolence. But our spine is made of steel. There is no turning back. It matters little if my life or the lives of colleagues should be sacrificed on this journey. Others will fill our sandals, and more will join and follow."[45]

Around the world Buddhists and non-Buddhists alike denounced the treatment of the Myanmar monks. Experts on

*Buddhist monks march in an antigovernment demonstration in Myanmar in 2007. Such protests sparked a violent backlash from the country's military, but the monks refused to cease their protests.*

Buddhism agree that the faith may well continue to face such assaults, along with other difficult challenges. Still, many of the experts are optimistic about Buddhism's future.

Former University of California scholar Lewis Lancaster, for instance, thinks that no matter what happens to individual Buddhists, the faith will continue to survive in Asia, where it originated. Meanwhile, he says, Buddhism will maintain its present steady growth in Western nations. Over time, its principles will be taught in growing numbers of Western schools, hospitals, and other institutions. In that way, he adds, Buddhism will likely reach a wider audience, gain increasing acceptance, and hopefully face fewer serious challenges. In the forefront of twenty-first-century Buddhism, he says, are groups

> that are helping to install Buddhist practices in [Western] places as widespread as South Africa, Australia, France, Norway, and Canada. . . . It is among Buddhist communities of Asian immigrants [in those nations] that we still find the support structures which have sufficient resources to establish Buddhist schools and institutions of higher education [in the West]. . . . My suggestion is that we are seeing the age old process of . . . Buddhism once again on the move, this time globally.[46]

# SOURCE NOTES

## Introduction: Buddhism: Religion or Philosophy?

1. Quoted in Wesley Baines, "Stories from a Monk: Find the Connection Between Inner Peace and Peace on Earth with Zen Master Thich Nhat Hanh," Beliefnet. www.beliefnet.com.
2. Quoted in Jordan Bates, "The 14 Mindfulness Teachings of Thích Nhất Hạnh's Zen Buddhist Order," Refine the Mind, May 7, 2014. www.refinethemind.com.
3. Nicholas Liusuwan, "Is Buddhism a Philosophy or a Religion?," *The Blog*, *Huffington Post*, May 31, 2016. www.huffingtonpost.com.
4. Liusuwan, "Is Buddhism a Philosophy or a Religion?"
5. Liusuwan, "Is Buddhism a Philosophy or a Religion?"

## Chapter One: The Origins of Buddhism

6. Quoted in Narada Mahathera, "The Life of the Buddha and His Greatness," UrbanDharma.org. www.urbandharma.org.
7. Quoted in E.J. Thomas, *The Life of Buddha in Legend and History*. London: Kegan Paul, 2003, pp. 50–51.
8. Quoted in Thomas, *The Life of Buddha in Legend and History*, p. 65.
9. Quoted in Lin Yutang, ed., *The Wisdom of China and India*. New York: Random House, 1955, p. 360.
10. Quoted in Will Durant, *Our Oriental Heritage*. New York: Simon & Schuster, 1997, p. 427.
11. Quoted in Buddha Dharma Education Association, "Life of the Buddha: The First Five Monks," 2008. www.buddhanet.net.
12. Quoted in Nancy W. Ross, *Three Ways of Asian Wisdom*. New York: Simon & Schuster, 1978, p. 82.
13. Sarvepalli Radhakrishnan, *Gautama the Buddha*. Bombay, India: Hind Kitabs, 1946, p. 1.

## Chapter Two: The Faith Spreads Far and Wide

14. Quoted in Ven S. Dhammika, trans., "The Edicts of King Ashoka," Colorado State University, 1993. www.cs.colostate.edu.

15. Quoted in Dhammika, "The Edicts of King Ashoka."
16. R.K. Mookerji, "Ashoka the Great," in *The History and Culture of the Indian People*, vol. 2. ed. R.C. Majumdar et al. New York: Bharatiya Vidya Bhavan, p. 74.
17. Azim Nanji and Sarfaroz Niyozov, "The Silk Road: Crossroads and Encounters of Faiths." Smithsonian Folklife Festival, 2002. www.festival.si.edu.

## Chapter Three: What Do Buddhists Believe?

18. John Makransky, "Buddhist Perspectives on Truth in Other Religions: Past and Present," Awakening Through Love. www.johnmakransky.org.
19. Quoted in Ross, *Three Ways of Asian Wisdom*, p. 80.
20. Buddhist Society, "Fundamental Teachings," 2017. www.the buddhistsociety.org.
21. Quoted in Yutang, *The Wisdom of China and India*, p. 361.
22. Sunthorn Plamintr, "The Five Precepts," UrbanDharma.org. www.urbandharma.org.
23. Plamintr, "The Five Precepts."
24. Durant, *Our Oriental Heritage*, pp. 431, 433.
25. Narada Thera, "Buddhism in a Nutshell," Buddha Dharma Education Association. www.buddhanet.net.

## Chapter Four: How Do Buddhists Practice Their Faith?

26. Gil Fronsdal, "Rituals in Buddhism," Insight Meditation Center. www.insightmeditationcenter.org.
27. Quoted in ReligionFacts, "Buddhist Monasticism." www.reli gionfacts.com.
28. ReligionFacts, "Buddhist Monasticism."
29. Buddha Dharma Education Association, "Meditation." www .buddhanet.net.
30. Alexander Berzin, "What Is a Mantra?," Study Buddhism. https://studybuddhism.com.
31. Quoted in *Lion's Roar*, "Do Buddhists Pray?," March 1, 2003. www.lionsroar.com.
32. Quoted in Buddha Dharma Education Association, "Buddhist Ceremonies." www.buddhanet.net.
33. Funeralwise, "Buddhist Funeral Service Rituals," 2017. www .funeralwise.com.

## Chapter Five: Buddhist Architecture, Sculpture, and Painting

34. Karen Shelby, "Buddhist Monasteries," Khan Academy, 2017. www.khanacademy.org.
35. Francis D.K. Ching et al., *A Global History of Architecture*. New York: Wiley, 2006, p. 169.
36. Peter Holleran, "Hellenic Buddhism and Buddhist Christianity." www.mountainrunnerdoc.com.
37. Deanna MacDonald, "Todai-ji," Khan Academy, 2017. www.khanacademy.org.
38. MacDonald, "Todai-ji."
39. Quoted in Dorling Kindersley, *Art: A World History*. London: Dorling Kindersley, 1999, pp. 168–69.
40. Department of Asian Art, Metropolitan Museum of Art, "Zen Buddhism," 2002. www.metmuseum.org.

## Chapter Six: What Challenges Does Buddhism Face in the Modern World?

41. Jeff Wilson, "Challenges and Opportunities: Speculations on a Buddhist Future," Patheos, July 5, 2010. www.patheos.com.
42. Wilson, "Challenges and Opportunities."
43. World Fellowship of Buddhists, "History," 2015. http://wfbhq.org.
44. The Dalai Lama, "Buddhism and Democracy," His Holiness the 14th Dalai Lama of Tibet,1993. www.dalailama.com.
45. Quoted in Human Rights Watch, "Burma: End Repression of Buddhist Monks," September 22, 2009. www.hrw.org.
46. Lewis Lancaster, "Buddhism: A Portable Religion in Australia," Buddhism & Australia. www.buddhismandaustralia.com.

# FOR FURTHER RESEARCH

## Books

Terry Barber, *Dalai Lama*. Edmonton, AB: Grass Roots, 2016.

Tammy Gagne, *Buddha*. Hallandale, FL: Mitchell Lane, 2017.

Color Smart, *Thai Buddhist Temples*. Charleston, SC: Amazon Digital Services, 2017.

Maura D. Shaw, *Thich Nhat Hanh: Buddhism in Action*. Nashville: Skylight, 2013.

Mark Thomas, *Buddhism*. Broomall, PA: Mason Crest, 2017.

## Internet Sources

Buddha Dharma Education Association, "Buddhist Ceremonies." www.buddhanet.net/funeral.htm.

Ven. S. Dhammika, trans., "The Edicts of Ashoka," Colorado State University, 1993. www.cs.colostate.edu/~malaiya/ashoka .html.

Ana Moriarty, "The History of Buddhist Art," *Widewalls*, June 5, 2016. www.widewalls.ch.

PBS, "Buddhism: An Introduction." www.pbs.org/edens/thai land/buddhism.htm.

*Stanford Encyclopedia of Philosophy*, "Buddha," February 3, 2015. https://plato.stanford.edu/entries/Buddha.

## Websites

**His Holiness the 14th Dalai Lama of Tibet** (www.dalailama .com). This official website of the Dalai Lama is full of colorful photos and links to videos, the latest news about the faith, and the Dalai Lama's Twitter, Facebook, and Instagram accounts.

**History of Buddhism, History World** (www.historyworld.net /wrldhis/PlainTextHistories.asp?historyid=ab77). A team of scholars led by historian Bamber Gascoigne put together this excellent general overview of Buddhism, which includes numerous links to articles about various subtopics.

**Tibetan Buddhism, BBC** (www.bbc.co.uk/religion/religions /buddhism/subdivisions/tibetan_1.shtml). One of the best sites of its kind on the Internet, this is a thoughtful, information-packed introduction to the history, philosophy, and political struggles of the Tibetan branch of Buddhism.

**World Buddhist Directory, Buddha Dharma Education Association** (www.buddhanet.info/wbd). This excellent website contains links to local Buddhist centers and organizations around the globe.

# INDEX

# PICTURE CREDITS

# ABOUT THE AUTHOR

Historian and award-winning author Don Nardo has written nu-merous books about the ancient and medieval world, its peoples, and their cultures, including the birth and growth of the major religions in those societies. Nardo, who also composes and ar-ranges orchestral music, lives with his wife, Christine, in Massa-chusetts.